John R Morrin II

Fractured Reflections

FRACTURED REFLECTIONS

Copyright © 2024 by John R. Morrin II

All rights reserved. No part of this publication may be reproduced, distributed, or transmitted in any form or by any means (including photocopying, recording, or other electronic or mechanical methods), without the prior written permission of the publisher, except in the case of brief quotations in a book review and certain other noncommercial uses permitted by copyright law.

First Edition

The opinions and or/views which are expressed in this work are solely those of the author and do not necessarily reflect the views or opinions of the publisher. Their appearance in this publication does not constitute an endorsement by Tactical 16 Publishing, its affiliates, or its employees. The contents and information conveyed herein is based upon information that the author considers reliable, but neither its completeness or accuracy are warrantied by the publisher, and it should not be relied upon as such. Tactical 16 Publishing hereby disclaims any responsibility or liability to any party for the contents of this publication.

This is a work of fiction. Names, characters, places, and events are either the product of the author's imagination or are used fictitiously. Any resemblance to actual persons (living or dead), events, or locations is entirely coincidental. No references made are intended to represent (and neither should they be inferred to represent) reality.

Cover design by Cindy Caulfield

Published by Tactical 16 Publishing

Colorado Springs, Colorado

www.Tactical16.com

ISBN: 978-1-943226-93-1 (paperback)

table of contents

Book One: Man's Best Friend   page 2

Book Two: Inverted Illusions   page 12

Book Three: Aqueous Transmissions   page 136

Book Four: Swan Song & Epilogue   page 186

acknowledgements

For my niece Makenzie: All the world is yours; and Riley too
For my sister: For strength and courage unmatched

book one

Man's Best Friend

Seven days had passed since my friend lay still when they had finally found us.

Those were the longest seven days of my life; and the darkest. None of this was supposed to happen, which makes it so hard for me to understand.

When we set out a week ago, it was going to be a day like many others we have had; a hike along one of the many trails that wind their way, turning this way or that, through our little part of the Rocky Mountains.

It was supposed to be a day like any other; a few hours heading through the woods, or up along a cliff, or down into the lush valleys below.

We drove further that day then we had ever driven before; hours passed by which only heightened my excitement. Walking these trails together was the one thing that saved me; it saved us both actually.

It has been a few years now since my friend and I first met; back home at the police academy. How quickly a bond was formed. And the bond was deep, and it was strong, and we shared a love for one another so fierce that we would have gladly sacrificed our life to save the other. Luckily it never came to that, and when it was time for me to hang it up, he came along with me too.

And though we both made it out in one piece, there were still wounds we suffered; the worst being below the surface. He could smile on the outside, but on the inside, he could only scream; and life for my friend became hard. I tried to do what I could to cheer him up, and for a time it would work, and he would be back. But soon then the pain would return; and I wept for my friend, though I never let him see.

Through this time, our bond never wavered.

After a while, we moved out of the city and headed West. I knew he needed space, and time, away from all of it. The pressures of life are great, and he bore many burdens, though I knew them not, for there are some things that just can never be shared; for the words aren't yet there.

After a while it felt like we could finally breathe again, and the crisp mountain aired filled me with hope for the future; a future with my best friend by my side.

Happiness is often fleeting, and though we live here in the moment, by the time we recognize it, it is already too late. And indeed, these days were the happiest of my life; and I hoped this for him too. But soon they were darkened.

The weeks passed and the same pain and anguish began to rise in my friend again; I could sense his weariness growing, but there was little I could do. I was heartbroken to watch him despair, and to sink so deep; watching a loved one battle alone is hard. What made it worse was my friend knew I was in pain with him, but this he only blamed on himself, which pushed him further from me.

I would give it all back to just share one more day.

. . .

A final glimpse of hope came when he had the idea for us to start going on long walks together. I was so happy. My friend wasn't ready to give up, he had a little fight left in him. And so, we started going for long walks together. And as the weeks went by, we started going further and further into the hills and the mountains around where we lived. We both felt alive, and when we looked at each other, all pain could be lifted for a moment.

I would give it all back to see my friend one more time.

It was supposed to be a day like any other. We packed up extra food and water and he told me we were going to go to someplace new and that we're going to be gone a little longer than normal. Maybe this is why he seemed more nervous then usual; something was off.

When we finally got there, it was well past noon and the sun was quickly falling behind the mountains around us. I wish I could have stopped us then, but against my better judgement he led us on.

It seemed as if my worrying was for nothing; he was smiling at me and things felt like they had before, but this was not to be the case.

We had been going for a few hours when we turned off a long-forgotten trail and entered into the wilderness. The shadows were long and the woods were getting dark, though the sun had some time yet to set.

I didn't like this, but I trusted my friend, and he led us on.

. . .

We stopped along a ridge overlooking a narrow ravine far below; the cliffs dropped off not far from us. There was something very serene about this place. It inspired silence and evoked beauty that couldn't be spoken into words.

We sat together in silence for a long time. I felt his hand rest on my shoulder and I felt at once all the days of our lives together. I was lucky to have shared so many wonderful moments with him, and this indeed was one of them. I think my friend was finally at piece.

The sun was sinking low.

After a time, he stood up to go get a better view of the ravine below. We shared a glance as he turned back as if to say one last thing to me; but his eyes jerked away, and as I watched helplessly, my friend stumbled and fell off the cliff.

We shared a glance…

I was at the edge of the cliff in an instant. And there I saw him; my friend laying still far below. I can't think. What just happened? He'll be okay when I get there. He has to be okay. The path down was hard, and I stumbled often. But I was now almost there; please hold on.

I finally reached my friend. My poor friend. He was breathing but it was shallow and faint. He was bloodied and bruised. I nudged him gently but he made no reply.

What should I do? I don't know what to do. Please someone help, anybody; please, I need help. But there was no one there.

. . .

I got down close beside him and tried to make him understand that he wasn't alone. I could never leave him alone. Not like this. No one should have to be alone like this.

When I felt all hope lost, he stirred and his hand came gently to my face. His eyes opened for a moment and we shared one last glance. My friend took his last breath and then was still. I felt his hand slide from me. How long I stayed there beside him I don't know. It was dark now, but I couldn't leave him.

There was only pain. No thoughts, no words, no memories; there was only pain.

I wept. I wept for my friend. For the happiness stolen from him all those years ago. For the life now bereft from him. I wept for my friend. For his family that he left behind. And selfishly, I wept for me.

Seven days had passed since my friend lay still when they had finally found us.

I never left his side; a place I was ready to die at. For with him went all of me.

His family took me in but the pain was too much. I died soon after. I don't think this is how it was supposed end. There were so many things in life left for us to do. But I know that we are now walking together again, my friend and me.

. . .

Just a man, and his dog.

   The End

However bitter it may be

book two
Inverted Illusions

I do not write… in hopes of being read
I do not write… in aims of pleasing anyone
I do not write… in order to be heard
I write… because I need to
I write… because I have something to say

Here is what I have to say…

Number One

If all was gray

She would be **red**

If all was red

Well

What then would she be

Number Two

If I ever happen to find love

Again

It would not be wholesome

For she

Has taken most of me

And I am afraid

Sadly

That neither her

Nor I

Shall ever be whole again

Number Three

Her love

The stormy seas

And I

The lone fisherman

And I will forever be haunted by the moment

I became lost at sea

Number Four

For you

There is nothing I would not do

For your love

There is little I can do

For your happiness

I must remain silent

Number Five

The universe has boldly brought us together

I do not believe this to be coincidence

Or chance

For it shook the very foundations of my planet

And whether or not it had been felt

By the rest of the world

Is irrelevant

For it still occurred

And it is still measurable

Measurable by science

And that science

That science

Is love

Number Six

I often wonder many things

Most of them never formulate into words

And more often than not

These are the most important thoughts we have

Imagine if all the people

Every single one of us

Shared just one of these thoughts

Just one

I wonder

Number Seven

I am not saying I am an adventurer

But I have done many things

And have travelled to many places

And through these experiences

I have learned

Among other things

More from my mistakes

And all my bad decisions

Then I have from all my successes

And yet

We are still only praised

For our victories

Rather than acknowledged

For our failures

Number Eight

Nothing in this cruel world

Is as loving as a mother's words

Or as warm as a mother's touch

And for that

I am grateful

To have walked this hurtful place

We call Earth

With a woman

As sweet

As the one

That I call mother

Number Nine

How is it fair

That you

Of all people

Can bring me to my knees

When I can stand up

To the very worst

That this world has to offer

But you

Are not of this world

For if you were

I would have found a way

Number Ten

As the skies darken

And this evil takes hold

What am I to do

Give up?

Never

I could not accept the defeat

That would cost me so much

For there are things to live for

Like her smile

Even just to see that smile

One more time

I would conquer anything

Number Eleven

If ever the Devil should call

And he will

Do not be afraid to answer

For it will be the most enlightening conversation

Of your life

And you will finish stronger than ever

And will never again be weary

To look fear in the eye

And speak

Bring it

Number Twelve

Am I the only one so near to insanity?

Every day I wonder if it will be the day

If it will reach the point

Where I can no longer

Hold it all together

I cannot be the only soul

Lost and confused

Wandering this harsh world

Alone

Or am I?

Number Thirteen

I have an unrelenting thirst for knowledge

I want to know all about humans

So hopefully one day

I will be able to understand

How she

A human

Can make me feel

They way that she does

Number Fourteen

Why are us humans

So afraid to reveal our feelings

When they are reflections of our soul

In its purist form

And

Are the closest things we have

To knowing who we truly are

Who are we?

Number Fifteen

As I lay there next to you

Holding your hand

You do not realize

That I am as far away from you

As the stars

That you so love to gaze at

Number Sixteen

You left me

So why can't you leave me in peace?

Everyday memories

Send me flying through time

Back to when

I once called you mine

Number Seventeen

Every person you meet

Is fighting a battle

Completely separate from your own

But

Not so different at all

We are all fit to handle

Exactly what happens to us in our lives

And when all hope is lost

And darkness is setting in

Remember

You were made to be able to make it through this

And you will make it through this

Number Eighteen

How is it that your lips say so little

But your eyes tell a never-ending story

A story of love

And life

That we are yet to enjoy

But still

You remain silent

Lying to me

Lying to your soul

Which is revealed to me

In every broken glance

Number Nineteen

What did I just say?

I think to myself

As I tell her words

That cannot be unheard

Words that will only lead her **down a path**

Which can only end in pain

I know I would have

Meant those words

If I was capable of

Feeling such ways as I

Promised to her I did.

What did I just say?

Number Twenty

Eyes cannot lie

They reveal a part of the soul

That is unknown to ourselves

It is a glimpse of the inside

That can only be seen from the outside

In an instant

When eyes lock

You connect with a person

And share a moment that is unlike any other

In the universe

Number Twenty-One

I have hundreds of conversations

Every single day

Yet very rarely do they ever

Formulate into words

They remain hidden from you

And everyone else

Why?

I am too afraid to reveal

The things I need to share the most

How long will I go on like this?

Number Twenty-Two

So many of my memories

Stay burned into my mind

As reminders of a time

To where I can never return

They haunt me

They taunt me

But above all

They remind me

Remind me why I am the way I am

Why I act the way I do

And for that

I relive these memories

As if replaying a familiar song

From long ago

Number Twenty-Three

In order to be timeless

All one must need to be

Is true

Number Twenty-Four

I am always divided

Internally conflicted

Never knowing what side to give in to

The good

Or the bad

The angry

Or the sad

Being down

Or being glad;

I always seem to choose the wrong one

The wrong choice for me

But the right one for those around

Who am I supposed to make happy?

Number Twenty-Five

She asks for the truth

And sadly

It is something I cannot tell her

Not for fear out of doing so

But simply for the fact

That I myself do not know it

It has been twisted

Obscured

Withheld from me

And covered up for so long

I cannot give her the truth

But I wish I could find it

But not for her satisfaction

But for my need to selfishly try to fix

The thing that is my life

A collection of feelings that I can't make sense of

The truth is so far away

And will always remain hidden from me

Number Twenty-Six

To be honest

I'm terrified

Scared to death

Of these new feelings

Emerging from a pit

Of only anger

And heart break

And the void that she once filled

Is now being filled

By an angel of pure perfection

And yet

I am unable to appreciate her fully

Because I somehow

Relate these feelings back to you

For I am quickly becoming her first love

Whereas you

Are still remaining mine

Number Twenty-Seven

I am not a child anymore

My eyes give away my weathered life

They are portals to a past that troubles me

But they remind me to be strong

I do not run from my past

Nor hide from it; though I used to

But my eyes reveal its' pain

My scars read like chapters in my book

Written across the lines on my face

A story so unique to me

That no one could ever fully understand

I am not a child anymore

Yet I feel the need to be held by another

Like that of a mother

And so your touch sends me traveling

Through time and space

Trying to get a foothold on one of the stars I pass by

I fear I have grown up too fast

And have somehow left a part of me behind

Never to be found again

I am not a child anymore

Number Twenty-Eight

Music is therapy for all of me

All of my problems

Its release into my nerves

Sooths and calms me

It amplifies my pain

And suffering

It drives my mind into an unrelenting

Feeling of understanding

And with my feelings personified

I can begin to make an attempt

At understanding them;

Music is life

Number Twenty-Nine

I regrettably rely on external stimulants

Anything to send my mind

To a place it cannot reach on its own

This doesn't necessarily mean drugs

Books, music, information, knowledge

Knowledge is a stimulant so very strong

It stimulates me to better myself

And keep pushing further and further

Number Thirty

You fool!

I shout

How can you believe time travel is not real

To open the pages

And to read the texts

Frozen in time

Emotions felt over centuries

Still alive today

Alive in the hearts

And minds

Of the reader

Ideas of long past

Brought to life

Time travel you say

How can you not see it

That way

Number Thirty-One

Night is a wonderful thing

Just as it is the opposite of day

Just as dark is the opposite of light

Night lets us be the opposite of ourselves

It turns our feelings into raw emotions

It allows us to reach a point in our souls

That is shielded during the day

Night is a wonderful thing

Number Thirty-Two

An extinguished fire is much easier to rekindle

Then it is to create a new flame entirely

It is the same with love, I have found

I would rather open a past chapter of my life

Then risking exposing my inner soul

To a new stranger

Giving one more person access to my inner insanity

So how can I tell her she has already lost me?

Or that she never truly had me

Number Thirty-Three

Missing

Number Thirty-Four

'What am I to do?'

She speaks

As I explain to her

I no longer love her

Or rather

I never did

For she is not the one

Whom I desire

I don't know how to love you

And how not to hurt you

"I'm sorry"

She only cries

And leaves me with hurtful words

That are all too true.

I'm sorry

Number Thirty-Five

These pages are stained

With a few brief stories of my soul

That are able to escape

If I let you read everyone

I wonder how your feelings of me would change

Number Thirty-Six

As I fall back into my old ways

I can't help but feel disappointed

How could I let myself slip

And as I'm falling down

There is no one reaching out to save me

Maybe because this time

I don't want to be saved

Or maybe

It is because this time

I know that I can't be

Number Thirty-Seven

I can look into your eyes

And see thousands of stars

Each telling me their own story

Each a part of your past

Your past that I once played a role in

Long ago

When you once said you loved me

And in your eyes

I find peace

Because I am looking at your beautiful

And imperfect soul

But it is perfect

Just like I always told you

Perfect because it matches mine

And combines into one with me

And as one we are complete

As one

We are perfect

Number Thirty-Eight

'I can't remember how long it has been'

'Too long' she says

'Why did you never come back?'

Tears are streaming down her face

And beginning to form in my eyes.

'I couldn't… I had to stay away to make sure this was real.'

She lost it all at that point

I don't blame her.

'What part of this didn't feel real?'

She leaves

I wonder if for good this time

I never knew if it was real

I guess I never will

Number Thirty-Nine

I can see the clouds lifting

A light begins to shine

Rays of hope cascading down

Filling my soul

Thinking to myself how lucky I am

So close to giving in

I have emerged focused and strong

However

Wounds have formed

Forged in the pits of my downfall

Never to be forgotten

Permanent reminders

Of who I once became

Number Forty

Every so often

Like cycles if the moon

Our love kindles

And grows anew

Then

Sadly

It wanes and disappears

Never resting on a permanent level

Never content

Never satisfied

Our love

Never satisfied

I wish one day

Me and her could find

Our own place in the sky

Number Forty-One

Reliving these old memories

And feeling those old feelings

I fall into old habits

Old addictions;

And new pain

New pain I have never felt before

Stuck in the grip of this choking air

I am suffocating

Gasping

Struggling to rise above this

I don't know if I will ever

Be truly free of this

I don't know if I ever

Want to be free of this

What would be left of me

If I didn't have this?

A blank smile, an empty stare;

I don't know who I am anymore.

Number Forty-Two

I guess you could call me a dreamer

For I am always dreaming of things that were

Or things that are yet to be

Never satisfied with the way things are

Always yearning for something more

I wish

I wish I could be happy

With the way things are.

Perhaps one day

Number Forty-Three

I wonder if the damage I have done

Is permanent

Will I have a normal life?

Do I even deserve a normal life?

I pray I do

I pray I can be normal

Again

Although

I don't know if I ever was

Completely normal

I wish I could ask you

If back then

You ever thought I was normal.

Number Forty-Four

My love for you is never failing

It will last for all eternity

If I could make you understand

One thing

It would be this

I will always love you

Always.

Number Forty-Five

So many came after you

And many before you

None do now remain;

I am afraid

None ever will.

You have taken me

Now why won't you take me for good?

I just want to make you happy

But you do not love me anymore

Yet you keep me by your side

Never letting me go

Why?

Why can't we let each other go

Is this meant to be?

Only time will tell.

Number Forty-Six

I wonder if you know what you mean to me

If you know that you are constantly

Keeping me in love with you

But you must know

You are constantly toying

And teasing

And refusing to let me go.

Why?

What do you want from me?

If you don't love me

Then please

Let me go

Just let me go

Please

Please.

Number Forty-Seven

I've finally made peace

Peace with this addiction

Never peace with you

However

I wish I could

Make peace with her

Make peace with my undying love

It never fails

Do you not understand?

Why do I shout this?

Only the blank stare in the mirror responds.

Why can't I come to peace with the fact

I will never have you

And that I never did.

Number Forty-Eight

Why is sleep

Someone I can never seem to meet

I am so longing for its presence

I am surrendering myself;

And nothing

Please

I beg you

Please let me know

I long for you

And for her

You both avoid me

Never accepting me.

Number Forty-Nine

I am a fraction of who I used to be

Yet you still see me for who I was

They have broken down every inch of me

And yet you still remain

But still, you won't accept what this is

You know as well as I

That this is fate

We are meant to be

That's why you won't let me go.

You hold onto me

Like an old, stained shirt

Torn

Wrinkled

But full of history.

Yet I would rather be that

Then the newest and most complete

And most whole

And sound man on this planet.

I like being your damaged

Hidden treasure

And that is what I am destined to be.

Number Fifty

'What kept you?'

'I've been away,

I couldn't stay here any longer.'

She has a look in her eyes

I have not seen before.

I don't know how to break it to her

'I left because of you'

She drove me to this life

That I must now suffer through

She has hollowed me out

Starting with my heart

And then devouring my soul.

My very essence

She looks at me

Tears hiding behind those soulful eyes.

'You should have never left.'

She leaves, and I can't help but wonder

Will I ever see her again?

Number Fifty-One

What am I doing?

Why do I do this to myself

Over and over

I drive myself down this unforgiving path

Of pain

And regret.

Number Fifty-Two

I'm sorry that we can't be together

But the time we spend apart

Will make it that much better

When we aren't.

Number Fifty-Three

I grow more complex

With every sleepless night

With every passing of the moon

I find myself

Entertaining new thoughts

And old habits

Both terrible and exciting

I tremble at the sight of day

And the thought of the light pains me

And just like every sunrise creeping in

My love for you creeps back

Into my mind

And fills my soul with wonder

And my heart

With pain.

Number Fifty-Four

I think

I am finally beginning

To understand

That I will never get what I want;

Everything I thought

This was going to be

Has turned out

To be

A false hope.

A wish I once prayed for

I am beginning to accept

That it is too late

And that it will never be

What I hoped

It would.

Number Fifty-Five

In my recent weeks

Of becoming self-obsessed

With my own downfall

A self-brought on addiction

A need to find meaning;

I have

Regrettably

Abandoned those most dear to me.

'I'm Sorry'

The words form in the depths

But can never truly exist

As a sound.

I can see the disappointment

Behind their sympathetic smiles.

I believe that I have permanently

Distanced myself from them

So entirely

That they will never accept me back.

Number Fifty-Six

There is no prescription

No cure

No help for this disease

My love-stricken soul

Is destined to stay this way forever

And for that

I am extremely grateful

For I am reminded

Every day

Every second

That love does exist.;

Yet somehow

I selfishly desire more

I am not content just merely knowing

Love exists in me

I need to know if it exists

In you

Also

Number Fifty-Seven

I wish you could see yourself as I do

Maybe then you would understand why

God I would do anything

To help you understand

The way I see you;

The beauty

The pain

The wonder

Hidden behind your eyes

The pure love

That radiates from your soul

Maybe then you would realize

Who you are

Not only who you are

To me

But also

Who you are to the world

A beautiful spirit

Number Fifty-Eight

Why do I continually have

This desire to take my mind

To places it has never been?

To stars it has never seen

And to highs I have never felt.

An addiction is growing inside me

And I am fearful

That I cannot fight it

Alone.

Number Fifty-Nine

Possessed by her soul

I find myself suffocating

Gasping

Desperately praying to see the light

To escape this darkness

That has overtaken me.

I no longer know who I was

Who I am now

Or who I am supposed to be.

Who am I?

Always asking the same question.

Number Sixty

I have become so painfully numb

Numb to everything

So many things that used to bring me joy

And happiness

Now pass invisibly through my soul

Barely eliciting an emotional response.

I can't derive this feeling

From a single event in my life

Rather

From a lifetime of disappointing setbacks.

And setbacks that left the people I love

Disappointed.

So, what does that make me?

A disappointment.

Number Sixty-One

I close my eyes

And like a flash of lightning

I go crashing through time.

And then it happens

I see you

And you smile at me

But she never smiles like anyone else

Anyone can move their mouth to form a smile.

However

With her

It was so much more

She can smile with her eyes

A smile from the soul

Beautiful and pure.

Now think about how many times

You close your eyes throughout the day

And then maybe you could understand my pain

And my love.

Number Sixty-Two

I long for strength

The sort of strength that generations of old

Once had

Oh to be strong like those men.

Although

I do not believe it to be my fault

Well

Not entirely my fault.

It is just the world we are living in today

And you know

It's a shame

Really.

Number Sixty-Three

Love is such a simple thing

Isn't it?

Just the basic idea of love is so simple

And yet

Can be explained in any number of ways

Hundreds upon hundreds

Of love filled souls.

Each telling their own love story

I suppose it is not so simple

After all.

Each love telling its' own complex history

Of heartbreak.

The ups and downs

Of every single love out there

Its' own unique song

Never to be sung

In the same way again.

Number Sixty-Four

My fall from grace has been everything but

I had never planned on giving in

But what was I supposed to do?

I was given no other choice

I have forsaken myself to a destiny

That offers little joy;

And less hope.

And it is all my fault

The path I am on is my own doing

My own struggle

My self-prescribed downfall

Unique to the choices I have made

That led me to this demise.

But if this is to be my undoing

Then I am going to change the rules.

I won't let you bring my down

And hold me under

This is not my permanent fall

Rather

A reminder

A reminder of who I am.

I have the strength within to defeat this

And I will.

Number Sixty-Five

The seconds of love are forever echoing

In the empty chambers of my soul

Never truly dying out.

I cannot silence the longing for a familiar love.

New love is too daring

Too frightening

The comfortable touch of a past lover

Number Sixty-Six

Absent

Number Sixty-Seven

I could never openly love you

At least

Not like all the others did

You were too special

Too pure.

They never understood your magnificence

I had to love you from afar

My feelings staying hidden in the dark.

That doesn't mean I never loved you

But rather that you

Never loved me;

And I never cared about that.

Admiring you from a distance

Was all I needed

Which means you

Were exactly what

I needed.

Number Sixty-Eight

Changing and evolving

Like the styles of writing

And form of my text

I am never content with where I am at.

The transition of my writing

Mirrors the growing of my soul

Although

While different on the surface

The underlying theme

Will always remain the same.

And I am unconventionally grateful

For the complex history

Told in the depths of my soul.

Sneaking out with every broken look

And every fractured smile

And every written word.

Number Sixty-Nine

I come back to these familiar places

But nothing is familiar to me anymore

Or maybe

I begin to realize

It's me that is no longer the familiar one

And it's almost as if the earth herself can understand

And she mourns for me

For the marring of my soul

Something which was not meant to be.

Number Seventy

My mind stumbles

Trying to find its own identity

At times it is as a cage

Locked inside

I can never escape it.

From the deepest pit

To the outermost thought

But yet

At other times

It is as a vast open plain

Where I can run free

And wander to the edges of thought

And time.

Freeing me from the real cage

That is my life;

The ultimate paradox

And I find it brilliant

And beautiful.

Number Seventy-One

Maybe it is blind ambition

Or maybe greed

Selfishness

Arrogance

False hope;

Or maybe it's just you.

Who knows what is driving me down this path

Which I am reluctant to admit that I desire

A truly unique life

That is all I am after…

Number Seventy-Two

I am continually being inspired by so many things

New books

New words

New songs

And tales

And romances;

New love and new heartbreak

New disappointment and new achievement

Always inspiring me

And forever changing me.

Number Seventy-Three

Whenever I am finally able to sleep

I am plagued by horrible nightmares

Things from which I cannot escape

No matter how hard I try.

And I can't help but wonder

Why?

Which event in my life has led me to this horror

Something I can never be rid of

And yet somehow

I am growing dependent of these nightmares

Almost longing for them

An escape from the present

No matter how dark.

Number Seventy-Four

I am unable to tell you

That I no longer desire you

When I look at you

I can no longer see you in my arms

And because I can't tell you that

I tell you nothing

I would rather have you hate me for that

Then hate me for telling you the truth.

Number Seventy-Five

I have constantly been longing for something more

I needed to feel I was here for a reason

That I had a higher purpose

To serve.

I can't help but think

That isn't the case anymore

Maybe I was meant to die on a battlefield long ago

Or maybe my destiny is still hidden from me.

Number Seventy-Six

How long must I search?

Can this feeling truly last forever?

I once thought my search was complete;

The moment I laid my lips on yours.

But you abandoned me

Left me to bleed out through the wounds

That you inflicted on my soul.

Number Seventy-Seven

I like to think of myself as a warrior

Physically

Mentally

Spiritually.

And I often find myself wishing I was a warrior from old.

Ancient

Powerful

Full of wisdom.

I would devote my whole life to that ideal

If it were still alive today.

Number Seventy-Eight

Just knowing the pain that you are in

Undeniably

Breaks my heart.

Understanding your despair

Tears at my very soul

You are so beautifully pure.

The universe should not allow one such as you

To endure so much heartache.

My only wish is to take that pain from you

And bear it myself.

Only to see you happy, once more.

Number Seventy-Nine

We are both so uniquely different

So in that sense we are both the same.

I wonder if by some miracle

You would open your heart to mine.

Compared to a wonderful angel like you

I would be a devil

The horrible life I have lived

Mirrored by the beautiful one of yours

Do you think we could work it out?

Heaven and Hell?

Number Eighty

I have developed a new passion for writing

Almost a need

I am able to say things I would not normally be able to say.

I can focus my mind

And free it of confusion

The words come to me

In a way I cannot explain.

The moment my pen touches a fresh piece of paper

I am able to let out a deep relaxing sigh.

And in that moment

No matter how brief

I feel as if everything

Will be alright.

Number Eighty-One

In another age

I could have been a great warrior

Leading men into battle.

A knight

A crusader;

Valiant.

Or perhaps a travelling mercenary

Never stationary

Always wandering this world in search of the next great adventure;

Something I am still searching for.

Maybe one day

I shall find it.

Number Eighty-Two

I've grown indifferent

To the fact that you love me.

I don't share those feelings with you

How can they be real

You don't even know the real me.

Not even a little bit

Not the part of me that writes these poems

And feels this pain.

You don't know me at all

Yet you claim this love.

A dumbfounded love that is meaningless

And false.

You can't mean it.

Number Eighty-Three

What is left of me

And what is left of my soul?

Which has been shattered beyond repair

You can't glue these pieces back together

They simply don't fall back into place

A piece broken from me

One by one by my own foolish decisions.

Piece after piece

Strewn across the floor

Like garbage in the street

Cast aside and left for dead.

Is that all my soul has become?

A pile of trash on the floor.

Number Eighty-Four

How could you so quickly go back to him?

Was everything you told me a lie

What happened to the girl

Who just yesterday

Was beginning to capture my heart,

To knowingly throw that away

For him

The one who drove you past the brink.

I have forever changed my thoughts of you

And to be honest

I wish you hadn't made.

Number Eighty-Five

The thought has crossed my mind

More times than I care to admit

But to get to that point

What must have crossed your mind?

What was possessing your heart

Suffocating your soul

You went where no one could follow

But left so many behind.

I can't help but wonder your thoughts and feelings

At the last breath you took.

Was it painful?

Or a relief?

Number Eighty-Six

Where do I go from here

I feel more separated from myself each passing day.

Almost as if I am fading

Disappearing.

Falling away from everything I know.

Things wash over me and leave no mark

Illicit no response

Only anger

Or fear

No happiness

No love.

I wish I could regain a sense of purpose

A sense of self-worth

Number Eighty-Seven

I just want to learn all of your secrets

Is that such a crime?

Why must you deny my affection

When you first told me you loved me

I didn't respond.

And now when I return your love

I am turned away?

Maybe it is what I deserve, after all.

Number Eighty-Eight

I am afraid

Terrified even

To try things

And do things I once did.

I am afraid I will no longer be able to perform them.

I am horrified of the thought of feeling

Nothing is familiar anymore

I feel like I have to start from scratch.

Number Eighty-Nine

I've grown so extremely paranoid

Of all my past decisions and actions

Coming back to haunt me.

Constantly looking over my shoulder so to speak

I leave a trail of heartbreak and destruction

Wherever I go

What am I supposed to do?

How can I outrun

All of my ghosts

There is nowhere to hide

These things

They catch up to me in my sleep

My nightmares are filled with the demons I cannot outrun.

And you want to know something?

I need them

I am addicted to closing my eyes

And seeing things I can't control from happening.

What the fuck is happening to me?

Number Ninety

Reading through these pages

I can track my life

The ups

The downs

The close calls

The times I thought I wasn't going make it.

The times I thought I was writing my last words

Or the times I was sure I was going to be okay.

I thought for sure I was free.

It's amazing to relive my moments

Page by page

Number Ninety-One

Death comes so sudden

And lately it has come in the shape

Of a horrible wave.

Taking out so many in its' path.

I wonder if it is something I can't feel anymore.

I know I should be sad

But I just feel empty instead

A storm cloud that refuses to rain.

It just keeps building up inside me.

Number Ninety-Two

In what way do you expect me to act?

After all this time, why now?

In my time of need

How do you appear when I need you most?

Then disappear right when it starts to feel the same

You can't just walk in my life

Stomp all over my soul

And then expect me to fix it again, on my own.

Number Ninety-Three

How many times must I come to your rescue?

Like a knight

A knight in shining armor

At your disposal.

And yet you dispose of me

Use me

Then go running back to the thing I just saved you from.

Number Ninety-Four

History has often been our strongest ally

Showing us the greats of our world

And how they did it.

But it is often overlooked

People never take into account

The countless number of pages in which all of life's questions

Are asked.

And more often than not

Answered.

Number Ninety-Five

I wonder if I will ever feel home again

I don't know if I can ever be content

With where I am at.

Feelings of comfort

And warmth and security.

I don't know if I can ever fully return.

Number Ninety-Six

I came to you when I thought you needed someone

When I thought you needed me,

You were so weak and fragile

On the edge of breaking and beyond all repair.

And for a time, I thought I was all you needed

And it seemed you believed it too.

For a time.

And just as quickly that I came to your rescue

You turned right back into your own demise.

And then you left me needing to be rescued

But no one ever came.

Number Ninety-Seven

How can I be mad at you for giving into your demons

When I continuously give into mine

How can I expect you to face them

Unless I face mine too.

Number Ninety-Eight

What has transpired

Surely can never die

For it lies locked away in vaults so deep.

And can only be opened in our moments of need.

But who is to determine

When our need is just right?

How will I know when I am ready?

And if not me

Then who?

Number Ninety-Nine

Forgotten

Number One Hundred

I grew up

And became so many things

I never wanted to be.

I don't know how this happened

But at some point, in life

Something changes us.

We see things differently

For some it may happen early

And for some it might happen too late.

But for all, it happens

I wish I could go back in time

To right before it happened

Just to look around

And take it all in.

How I felt

How it felt to be alive

What my biggest worries were

Breathe in the air of innocence

Because that would be the last time

I ever felt that way.

Number One Hundred and One

I hope one day I can find what I seek

This feeling I just can't seem to place

What is my dream I am so desperately chasing?

If I don't know, how can I be sure I am on the right path?

I blindly jump into the unknown

In hopes that I will stumble onto some greater purpose.

Some true calling

What I was born to do

As sure as the sun

Chases the moon

I too chase

Although

I do not know what I am chasing.

Number One Hundred and Two

It seems I have lost my way

It seems everyone has lost their way

We as a people must get back to the things we now take for granted

Nature

The stars

Simple interactions with another.

In every aspect of our lives

Technology has taken over.

Nobody reads

Nobody writes

Our days are spent looking into screens.

When will we get back to being human

Interacting with the world

Instead of destroying it.

We must get back to who we are

Regardless

At least I will stay true

To who I am.

Number One Hundred and Three

This chapter of my life is coming to a sudden close

I have felt every emotion I have ever known.

Felt things I never thought were possible

I have accomplished things far beyond my hope

And I fell lower than I ever wanted to go.

Looking back

Over the past few years

I cannot help but reminisce

Friends come and gone

Lovers lost

Traveling the world

Just to find myself in faraway places

To know I will never live this double life again

Is a weird feeling.

But looking ahead

Riles up a whirlwind of emotions.

I am excited to see where my life will lead.

The End

The previous verses were written between 2013 and 2015 while deployed overseas, and appear in the order in which they came to be.

Thank You

book three

Aqueous Transmissions

α ~ alpha ~ α

The sea is vast and terrible and large

Seemingly endless; bound to no shore.

To think of all the life that lived there

But man came and he made that life no more.

My sails broke off and the mast came down

Nothing left in sight I can see no shore.

Lost at sea I begin to drift away; floating on and on I go

Until their memory of me is no more.

β ~ beta ~ β

A wave becomes and crashes; the majesty and power repeats

Over and over he crashes; none truly appreciate this feat

Trying to escape the storm; your ship the sea defeats

None are safe, no quarter given; no chance left to concede

The wind blows as the thunder crashes; there are no moments of peace

A lighthouse braces, the water crashes; your only moment to breathe

Lightning cuts in half the storm; the rocks they shatter against the sea

The lighthouse rumbles; he weathers the storm; the majesty and power repeats

γ ~ gamma ~ γ
Raise your sails and begin the journey

To destinations
Most unknown

Rising as the king amongst his court
The wave mounts
And claims his throne

δ ~ delta ~ δ

Lost at sea I drift away

I've lost my sails they've blown away

Where is the lighthouse? It washed away

Thunder approaches; clear skies away

Only wreckage here and the world is away

Forever lost at sea my mind forever away.

ε ~ epsilon ~ ε

The song of the sea rings forever in my ears and turns my eyes and feet to the West

Where are kings of old and legend and lore; mankind's very best

And to the West I hear a calling, pulling me towards a destiny I do not yet know

But this I do know, that surely I must go, go to what awaits me in the West.

The trickle of the stream, the snowflake falls, water crashes and the water falls

One drop in the ocean, indistinguishable from the rest

Yet still I hear the sea calling, urging me to the West.

ζ ~ zeta ~ ζ

I find myself lost at sea; I am adrift.

Do I even want to be found?

Who can say.

The anger that once consumed me now seems more like a gift.

The devil creeps silently and cold; are these my final days?

Who can say.

Where am I going? I can't seem to remember my path.

Are memories left best stored and shut away?

Who can say.

The wave I now see approaching; I will face it head on and let the sea claim me.

Perhaps this is the better fate.

Who can say.

η ~ eta ~ η

A wave mounts and strides ashore…

        …Crashing and falling like never before

The seasoned veteran; white adorns his hair…

        …Pushing and pulling, outlasting the storm

As the water recedes, we entreat to its' wake…

        …But when the sea recedes most drastically

Be careful of your fate…

        …The eye of the storm is but a brief respite

Praying that you survive, you pray to outlast the night…

        …When dawn comes and you emerge unscathed

Be wary of the dead…

…Those who could not be saved

θ ~ theta ~ θ

Sailing on my vessel, I am on a voyage at sea; destined to worlds unknown.

A new land to settle, a new town to build; a new world free to roam.

I step to the rails; and all thoughts now disappear.

Something tugs at me, and dares me to go overboard, over the rails.

A stronger tug now in the direction I do not wish to go.

With opportunity on the horizon, why now do I yearn to jump?

What starts at a whisper now roars into a scream!

Jump…

I jump

I am, but not all, is lost.

ι ~ iota ~ ι

Where the ocean and sky meet
This is where it happens
The blending of the encircling currents
And encompassing waters
Stretching on and on
Across the void.

ϰ ~ kappa ~ ϰ

Take away the flesh and the soul yet still remain

Strip away the armor still a knight stands true

The husk of a man does whither and fade; armor rusts and eats through;

What is left?

The essence of life.

As above so below and so shall we all must die.

And upon death we may return anew; as a breeze in the sky;

Or as the blade of grass graced by the dew.

λ ~ lambda ~ λ

A way of being most right; dreaming to live amongst people in God's light.

One with nature and one with the sky; the Embera people and their Ancore is life.

On the waters and off the land they have no heed for money; a life most fulfilling.

Have we lost our way? Bound by block and steel.

Barefoot in the mud, I again now feel a life most real; the true way to be.

Alas, I set sail and leave them all behind; but forever they remain with me

In a small corner of my mind.

μ ~ mu ~ μ

Once again I find myself on foreign soil

Exploring mankind's great feats and toils.

South America today, perhaps another world tomorrow

A land beyond and far away; perhaps a land much further.

Traveler I am yet explorer I wish to be

Perhaps in another life I could be free to roam

The lands and waters unknown.

Maybe, it just may be.

v ~ nu ~ v

The sea will fold itself in two

Devouring ships, mast, and crew.

Pulling all down to the darkened deeps

Down to Hell's locker.

Never underestimate the water

The majesty; the power.

~ xi ~

There is a time at sea in the dead of night, where there is nothing to see and there is no light.

A wall of black as cold as death; impenetrable.

Being lost here means no coming back, to survive is to cheat death.

Forever after the reaper and thou are inseparable, abiding his time to collect the toll you owe. How many times can you cheat death yet still remain?

Death is the master don't become the pupil, forever to obtain a life everlasting.

This fate I choose not for myself as when my time comes, and come it shall

The reaper himself shall guide me home.

o ~ omicron ~ o

The lady in white occasionally I have visited as is my wont.

More wrong than right, the shadows creep in and keep me from the light.

Five lines down, snowblind, and the night has only yet begun.

The feeling seeps its way in; perhaps one more then I am done.

Pacing to and fro the mania sets in.

Following along, my ducks all in a row.

How far this time shall I go?

Snowblind.

Cut the tether and disregard the storm; I cut my sails.

Lost, I am forlorn; again, my discipline fails.

The opposite of north I find myself somewhere south, down in my Hell.

Line after line after line. What part of space will I end up this time?

The dark vast emptiness inside of my mind.

π ~ pi ~ π

A ship now cuts the sea
Mania returns
A place you should never go
And a place most never know
Visiting peoples
Removed from the world;
I wish to stay among them
And remain.
Mania returns
I travel to space
I find myself again alone
A distant world;
A foreign place.

ϱ ~ rho ~ ϱ

Fire, smoke and black night.

The dark itself is more than just a lack of light.

It consumes and devours all.

Turns cold even the hearts of the bravest men proud and tall.

An unlight feast; it preys on the souls

Of those she ensnares in their mind's hell; a dark black hole.

The moon recedes and leaves you blind

Blind to the light when all is black as night.

No stars; Neither distant and dim nor close and bright.

It is not safe here, don't stray far –

A moment too late, now lost you are.

σ ~ sigma ~ σ

Mountains raised and oceans delved, the Maker made all you see before you; Himself.

For how else could the flower be explained, or the eagle high in flight.

A cloud in the sky where winds of the sea blow and the wandering albatross free to roam.

A million stars above, are we truly alone?

The first or the last; alpha and omega.

When my day of judgment comes; steadfast, I pray that I shall pass.

τ ~tau ~ τ

I hear my ancestor's whisper; they question my actions.

The only thing worse than my failures, I deem; is indeed a lack of action.

Choosing not to choose is a choice of its very own.

Which God do you answer to? Will you then bow down before the throne?

Falling up I come crashing down.

He lifts me up; He sets me down.

How then could I not believe?

The beauty of clouds and the calm of the seas.

From the torment inside, a brief moment of peace.

υ ~ upsilon ~ υ

Drip

Drip

Drip

Drip

The bucket fills

The bucket spills

Inch

By inch

By inch

By inch

The world steps

It approaches death

ϕ ~ phi ~ ϕ

However clear the waters be

The sun itself does never reach

The darkest depths of oceans deep.

The surface feigns and sues for peace

While dark unknowns beneath it creep

A world apart in oceans deep.

What is that I see?

What could it be

A world of dreams under the sea;

To this I must now swiftly leave

And see what lies below for me.

Its dungeons deep and far below

To rocky peaks where white falls snow;

A vision appears to me I see

A world apart beneath the sea.

χ ~ chi ~ χ

The rising tide

Swelling inside

Demons abide

No where to hide

Sinking; subside

Tell them I tried

Don't tell them I lied

Please help, revive

Too late; I've died

ψ ~ psi ~ ψ

The time is near

Coming to an end

The river does run

The river does bend.

The end has come

The end is here

Too late to run

Dark visions appear.

Water rising

I sink beneath the surface

My life wasted

A failed purpose.

ω ~ omega ~ ω

The storm lessens
The waters recede
Grace restored
God's Grace received

book four
Swan Song & Epilogue

'The Door'

A door appears, at first so plain and nothing more

But then I see

And as I draw near

I see this door as something else and something more.

I view the door from the outside

Unable to see the other side

But I remain afraid

To put myself within

And see myself inside.

Unable to turn away

Yet now I cannot press forward

My momentum stayed

And indeed, this way it stayed

Drawing to a close

This dark winter day.

It is but a door, a door and nothing more

All my life I have but passed right through

And have done so, so many times before.

A door is here that lies before

I hesitate and stay a moment longer

Now stretching seconds more

Yet I remain unable to commit myself

And step inside

To step inside this door.

A door appears at first

A door and little more

But now I see this door, yes, *this* door

As something more

And where once it solely stood

Now indeed stands something **more**.

Long I sat and pondered this

I wondered and implored

Standing in between alone

Like standing on the shore.

Wait!

What's that I hear, is that a tapping at my door?

What noise has now appeared

I swear I've heard it once before

Silence now returns

No more rasping on my door.

So, knowing this, but knowing nothing more

I decided once again to wait

So, wait I did and stay I did

I sat hiding at my door.

Finally, I will discuss this no more

I reach to pass through;

My hand is stayed

Only for a moment.

What's that?

I hear a sound

Coming from the other side

The other side of my door.

Faint; less than a whisper.

I press against the door my ear

And slowly I begin to hear

"Why has he not yet passed through?

It is but such a simple chore."

"Silence, quiet! He might hear you"

A flash; clarity.

I see briefly through the veil upon my eye.

Now, as yin and yang

I see both sides

Yet I remain afraid

Afraid to put myself within

And be myself inside.

"Hello" I say "Who's there?"

Nothing.

No response, no sound

Nothing more.

Not one single whisper I hear

Only the rust cold steel of the door.

I reach to pass through; trembling

"Not yet" I declare.

I pause

A moment turns longer

The moment drags on

Frozen in time I feel the abstraction in my mind.

I see clearly from my beginning

And through my end

On the other side is as what lies hidden

Far beyond the bend.

Hidden from eyes

Until through it you descend.

I reach to pass through

· · ·

Tap tap tap…

Now in the air my hand is stayed

What is that? I wonder

What is that sound on my door

"Who's there?" I declare

"Don't lie to me, now, for I know that you are there!"

Nothing; silence.

"Answer me, I say! Why are you here, tapping at my door."

Nothing; silen –

"Your door?" I hear

My hand frozen, trembling

Inches from my door.

"You lay claim to that which you cannot pass through?

How could such a thing even belong to you?"

I startle

"But if this be the case, then I declare

That it is now my door too.

What say you?"

Recognizing my folly

I speak more quickly

"Forgive me, for I spoke in haste

Let us live peacefully here

And share this place.

On either side we each

May have our space.

So, let's have peace

For here I wish to stay."

Nothing; Silence.

"Why stay there

When you don't yet know what lies on my side?

For on my side, surely you can abide.

Here I have no care for time

Nor money

Neither sickness nor death here

Shall you find."

What an idea; no

I shake it from my head.

"You tempt me, friend

But here I will reside

At this place here;

Which lies on my side.

My side of the door."

Have I overreached my hand? I pull it back

· · ·

"Again, you speak as if you know all the truth
Do all the answers then lay hidden
Deep inside of you?"

"That is not what I meant
And you know that, too.
But why should I leave here?
Yes; and put my trust in you?"

"As you said it, so it was doomed.
And this now do I declare to you!
Stay there if you wish
On your side of the door
But I will not ask again
Not once; no more.
And never again shall I approach you
At your door."

"Wait!" I exclaim
Nothing; no more.
I reach my hand
Yet again my hand is stayed.
Why is it such
That I cannot escape
And cannot leave this place?

"The grass is surely greener"

I whisper aloud

But still…

What remains beyond this door

Lays hidden in shroud.

"Harden yourself"

I say more proud

I reach out my hand

And pass through

Somehow.

What lies beyond

Is now no more

For yours and mine

Are separate doors.

Will you go or will you stay?

Pulling and pushing yourself

Each and every way

But to you, this I say

As I close my door

Never to open again

Nevermore;

Staying still or pressing on

Whichever path you explore

Throughout your life

You likely shall come to many doors.

To open is risky

As it is risky too to stay

Which will you choose?

What will be your fate?

And how will you know

If you win or lose?

A door appears

It is nothing more.

'Arbitrary titles'

Chasing Them Away

Never Late

A Ripple in Time

Day Dreaming of Clouds

The King of the Jungle

A Fireside Chat

Whispering Water

Running Stream

The Dilemma

When the Hour Strikes Midnight

Owner of a Broken Heart

Turning a Page

A Quarter Short

Slipping Away

Trapped Inside

A slight Breeze

Around Again

This Way or That

Pulled Down Low

Far East Memories

Tranquil Power

How the Bull saw it

Go and See

Spiritual Ascension

One at a Time

Déjà Vu

Déjà Vu

In the House of the Rising Sun

Hiding in the Shadows

Deeper in the Mist

Around in my Head

Dragons in the Night

Showing Your True Colors

Temperature Rising

Could This Be

What I Deserve

Floating Around

An Empty Room

So Many Thoughts

Changing my Views

Getting Myself into Trouble Again

The End

'The Telling pt. 2'

The deeper we go the darker you will find; be weary of yourself and weary of your mind

The tale continues as most tales do; looking back through the ages we hasten to find the truth

To start again we must dig deeper, clear and present dangers, the lost all fear the seeker

Picking up the story, can you recall where we left off? It's time we take this further, are you ready to set off?

Hitler rose and Stalin towered; Mussolini pretended while the West all cowered

Reclaim the first, partition the second; a secret solution, the devil hath beckoned

The struggle was told but the world seemed to ignore; with cowardice and ignorance, fear spreads evermore

What can be told of the ovens, that smoked in the dark night

'I was just following orders' a lie told that sounds most right

Do not be fooled, for it lies within you; do you think you would hide Anne Frank? I doubt that would be you

I don't mean to be harsh, but history keeps the score; with so many goose-stepping, courage walks right out the door

Bergen-Belsen is a name you don't know; yet the Hollocaust happened less than a hundred years ago

How many died? Who can say a number; starved beyond deprivation, dying of thirst and hunger

Barbarossa steamed ahead and mowed the flowers down; all for a namesake placed onto a town

Alone in his bunker, the world burning all around; enemies closing in, Berlin tumbled to the ground

What Nuremburg taught us, are things we can't ignore; ignorance isn't innocence, the train-master's feet swung above the floor

We can now switch gears, for there is more than one evil here; though Hitler's claim is first, he was but the tip of the spear

Stalin and Mao, how many million dead; All for a cause, just leaping ahead

Red waves of death, now ripple on our shores; the weak remain silent while communism grows more

And as I learn more from the lessons of the past; the more I fear that these days will be our last

Well, you've come this far, dare to go a little further? Hollocaust or Genocide, is murder just murder?

The rape of Nanking, one neighbor turned on the other; Beyond the absence of Love, Cain killed Abel, his own brother

Imagine yourself the sinner, for you are from the saint; Visions of Hell before you, paradise lost; the Devil waits

There is wickedness in you, a shadow most deep; don't fear the darkness; your soul soon, grim shall reap

Perhaps these words are more than you can bear; will the world show you sympathy? I doubt that they would care

One part of the whole, still many passages remain; your mind in dark thought, yes, deep now in Hell's domain.

'The Shadow'

Lurking there beneath the surface
I fear your presence near
What now here could be your purpose
My mind it fills with fear

Inching towards me; creeping close
Why must you trap me here
The raven sees me and he crows
The end I feel is near

My wicked shadow haunting me
To temptation I now steer
My reflection laughs so tauntingly
Evil does now appear

'Footprint of a Sinner'

An earth-bound chasm presents in my path

Too vast to elude or escape

No route to turn back, retreating

Descending is against my will

But still this choice is

The choice that is made

No trail to guide me through

A maze of rock and stone

Sheer walls

Underneath the shadow of the sun.

An earth-bound chasm presents in my path

Now escaping I turn astray

And see before me the sun

And the rays sent before him

Now further I descend

More troubles on the mind

I think of things left and forgotten

They lie below the earth and decay

Rotten they are to the core.

'Fractured Reflections'

. . .

I see myself and I see that I am broken

I wish I always told the truth but surely I've misspoken

A vision of me that is good is something I have no hope in

A life of trouble and disarray is what has been foreboded.

The armor pierced and dented can yet still remain unbroken

But the lies I've told that hurt the most can never be unspoken

The world lost trust and your fellow man you now have no hope in

A life of pain and misery is what has been foreboded.

A shackle rusts it breaks in two, forever he lies broken

You think you're free, the lies they told, you echoed freely spoken

Now my friend is an enemy and you are someone I have no hope in

A vision of me I see will shatter just as has been foreboded.

'The Final Cost'

Through the third rise and fall, history revealed all

Names best not forgotten shall now here be told

A thing most evil, most treacherous to behold

The order of death was at the head

A wickedness takes hold.

. . .

Theresienstadt Ghetto can be where we start

At least 33,000 how's that for a start?

The same can be said of Dachau and Bergen-Belsen

With over 30,000 each more.

So many at Chelmno, truly a horror

320,000 murdered, truly a horror.

Majdanek 360,000

Mauthausen 120,000

Sobibor 250,000

Belzec 600,000

Auschwitz 1.2 Million Liquidated

Yes, that is the word that they used.

Do you understand these numbers?

Do you recognize these names?

The Warsaw Ghetto

Fighting back in vain

What about Westbork

Or Vaivara?

Or Stutthof?

Or Sered?

Or Sachsenhausen?

Ravensbrück.

Plaszow.

Neuengamme.

Struthof.

Koldichevo.

Kaiserwald.

Janowska.

Flossenburg.

Drancy.

The horror.

The horror ..

The horror…

The horror….

The horror…..

The horror……

One for every million

Oh, the horror

the end

; but there is always an after…

about the author

John Morrin is an avid reader and lifelong student. He is a passionate writer who is dedicated to creating an authentic anthology of poetry, blending together themes of psychology, philosophy, theology and beyond. In his debut work, John weaves together his experiences from his time before, during, and after his service in the Marine Corps; with the current, everyday struggles he has faced due to the invisible wounds he suffered.

John served his country honorably by enlisting in the United States Marine Corps at 19 years old, where he had five overseas deployments, totaling three and a half years spent on foreign soil. He has been both the warrior and the tradesman, the storyteller and the fool. John currently resides in Ohio with his beautiful wife, who has been the most instrumental part of his recovery, and their three dogs: Athena, Titan, and Bowie.

About the Publisher
TACTICAL 16

Tactical 16 Publishing is an unconventional publisher that understands the therapeutic value inherent in writing. We help veterans, first responders, and their families and friends to tell their stories using their words.

We are on a mission to capture the history of America's heroes: stories about sacrifices during chaos, humor amid tragedy, and victories learned from experiences not readily recreated — real stories from real people.

Tactical 16 has published books in leadership, business, fiction, and children's genres. We produce all types of works, from self-help to memoirs that preserve unique stories not yet told.

You don't have to be a polished author to join our ranks. If you can write with passion and be unapologetic, we want to talk. Go to Tactical16.com to contact us and to learn more.

All of Tactical 16's books are available on our online bookstore, T16Books.com. Visit it today to see more books from our selection of authors and to find a new adventure to read!

Milton Keynes UK
Ingram Content Group UK Ltd.
UKHW020123221024
449869UK00010B/421